THE LAUNDRY
ENTREPRENEUR

A Guide to Launching Your Home-Based Laundry Business with Minimal Capital

JEFFREY FERON

CONTENTS

INTRODUCTION

In a world where life moves at an ever-accelerating pace, where time is a precious commodity, and where the pressures of daily living demand efficient solutions, one age-old necessity remains steadfast—clean, fresh clothing.

As long as humanity wears fabrics, the laundry industry stands as a testament to both the inevitable reality of laundry and the boundless potential for entrepreneurial spirit.

Enterprising minds are continually seeking innovative avenues to merge tradition with modernity, and the laundry business is no exception.

This book, "Laundry Entrepreneur: A Guide to Launching Your Home-Based Laundry Business with Minimal Capital," is your comprehensive road map to tap into this timeless demand, transform your home into a bustling laundry hub, and launch a successful venture with just a modest budget.

Whether you dream of owning a thriving laundry empire, making your entrepreneurial mark, or simply creating an additional source of income from the comfort of your home, you're about to embark on a journey that will unveil the strategies, insights, and secrets of launching and running a home-based laundry business with minimal capital.

Through these pages, we'll unravel the mysteries of stain removal, reveal the art of fabric care, and dive into the intricacies of logistics, all while crafting an enterprise that harmonizes the traditions of laundry with the modernity of business.

We'll explore the methods to nurture loyal customers, expand your reach, and embrace eco-conscious practices to reduce your carbon footprint.

This guide isn't just about cleaning clothes; it's about cleaning up in business. From the laundry novices to those seasoned in the art of stain removal, this book will serve as your mentor, guiding you through the ins and outs of running a successful home-based laundry business.

Prepare to embark on a transformative journey. By the time you've turned the final page, you'll be equipped with the knowledge, tools, and inspiration to wash away the barriers to success and watch your laundry business flourish, turning your home into a thriving hub of cleanliness and profit.

The Essential Need for Laundry Skill and Training in Your Laundry Business

Embarking on any business venture, especially a home-based laundry business, requires a combination of passion, determination, and a well-rounded skill set.

While the idea of running a laundry business may seem straightforward at first glance, the truth is that success in this field often hinges on the level of expertise, knowledge, and training you possess.

Here are compelling reasons why acquiring laundry skills and training is paramount before launching your laundry business:

1. Quality Control:

- The primary goal of a laundry business is to deliver clean, well-maintained clothing to your customers. Skill and training are fundamental in achieving consistent quality.

- Understanding fabric types, proper care, and stain removal techniques ensures that every garment you handle receives the attention it deserves.

2. Customer Satisfaction:

- Happy, satisfied customers are the lifeblood of your laundry business. Without the necessary skills, you risk disappointing clients with damaged, poorly cleaned, or improperly handled clothing.

- Trained laundry professionals can provide exceptional customer service by addressing specific requests and concerns effectively.

3. Stain Removal Expertise:

- Stains come in all shapes, sizes, and degrees of stubbornness. A comprehensive knowledge of stain removal techniques is essential for maintaining the integrity of garments.

- Training equips you with the ability to tackle a wide range of stains, from wine spills to oil marks, enhancing your reputation for reliability.

4. Equipment Mastery:

- The laundry business involves various equipment, from washing machines to dryers and ironing tools. Knowing how to operate, maintain, and troubleshoot these machines is crucial.

- Training ensures that you can efficiently manage and extend the lifespan of your equipment, saving you money and preventing downtime.

5. Efficient Workflow:

- A trained laundry professional understands the value of efficiency and workflow optimization. Proper training can help you establish streamlined processes for sorting, washing, drying, and folding.

- Efficiency not only reduces operational costs but also allows you to handle a higher volume of laundry.

6. Eco-Friendly Practices:

- Modern consumers increasingly value eco-conscious businesses. Training can provide insights into sustainable practices, including the use of eco-friendly detergents, water conservation techniques, and energy-efficient laundry procedures.

- Demonstrating a commitment to environmental responsibility can set your business apart in a competitive market.

7. Knowledge of Regulations:

- Depending on your location, there may be specific regulations and health codes governing laundry businesses. Training ensures that you are aware of and in compliance with these requirements.

- Ignorance of regulations can lead to fines, legal troubles, and reputational damage.

8. *Continuous Improvement:*
- The laundry industry is ever-evolving, with new cleaning techniques, equipment innovations, and customer preferences emerging. Regular training allows you to stay updated and adapt to industry changes.

- Learning should be an ongoing process to keep your business at the forefront of industry standards.

In summary, investing in laundry skill and training is an essential foundation for your laundry business's success. It not only ensures the quality of your service but also contributes to customer satisfaction, equipment maintenance, efficiency, and adherence to regulations.

Ultimately, a well-trained laundry entrepreneur is better equipped to thrive in a competitive market and provide a service that clients can trust and rely on.

Chapter 1

Research and Planning

A. *Market Research:*

1. Identify Your Target Market: Start by understanding who your potential customers are. Are you targeting busy professionals, college students, families, or a combination of these? Understanding your target market will help tailor your services to their specific needs.

2. Competition Analysis: Investigate the existing laundry services in your area. This involves finding out how many laundromats and other home-based laundry services there are, what services they offer, and their pricing. This will help you identify gaps in the market and determine how to differentiate your business.

3. Pricing and Services: Research the average pricing for laundry services in your area. This will give you insights into setting competitive yet profitable prices. Explore the range of services offered by competitors and consider what unique services you can provide.

4. Location Considerations: Assess the accessibility of your location. A home-based business should ideally be situated in an area with a target customer base within a reasonable distance.

5. Demand Analysis: Determine the demand for laundry services in your area. Consider factors such as the local population, the presence of students, professionals, and the availability of laundry facilities in the vicinity.

B. *Business Plan:*

1. Business Concept: Define your business concept in detail. What types of laundry services will you offer (washing, drying, ironing, folding, alterations, etc.)? Will you specialize in any specific niche, like eco-friendly laundry, stain removal, or quick turnaround?

2. Startup Costs: Estimate the initial capital required to start your home-based laundry business. This should include costs for equipment, supplies, permits, and any renovations needed for your laundry space.

3. Legal Considerations: Determine the legal structure of your business, such as a sole proprietorship, LLC, or corporation. Investigate local business licensing requirements and ensure you comply with health and safety regulations.

4. Operating Costs: Calculate the recurring costs, including utilities (water, electricity), laundry supplies (detergents, fabric softeners, etc.), and any marketing expenses.

5. Pricing Strategy: Develop a pricing strategy based on your research findings. Set competitive prices that also ensure profitability. Consider whether you'll charge per pound, per service, or with package deals.

6. Marketing and Promotion: Outline your marketing plan. This should encompass your branding, online presence (website and social media), local marketing efforts, and strategies to build and retain customer loyalty.

7. Financial Projections: Create financial projections, including revenue forecasts and expense estimates for the first few years. This will help you understand when you can expect to break even and start making a profit.

8. Sustainability and Eco-Friendly Practices: If you plan to incorporate eco-friendly practices into your business, outline how you'll do so, and consider how these practices can be integrated into your marketing and branding.

9. Growth Strategy: While you may start from home with limited capital, think about your long-term growth strategy. If the business succeeds, how do you envision expanding? Will you invest in more equipment, open additional locations, or offer pickup and delivery services?

A well-researched and detailed business plan serves as a roadmap for your home-based laundry business. It not only helps you understand the market and competition but also prepares you for the challenges and opportunities that may arise as you start and run your business.

Adjust your plan as needed, especially in response to changes in the market or your business's growth.

Chapter 2

Legal and Regulatory Considerations

Starting a home-based laundry business requires adherence to various legal and regulatory requirements to ensure your operation is compliant and lawful. Below are key considerations:

A. *Business Structure:*

1. Select a Legal Structure: Decide on the legal structure of your business. Typical choices consist of a sole proprietorship, partnership, limited liability company (LLC), or corporation. The choice you make will impact your personal liability, taxation, and reporting requirements.

2. Business Name: Choose a unique and memorable business name. Ensure it's not already in use by another business in your area. You may need to register your business name depending on local regulations.

B. *Permits and Licenses:*

1. Local Business License: Contact your local city or county government to determine if you need a business license to operate a home-based laundry service. The requirements may vary depending on your location.

2. Home-Based Business Permits: Check with your local zoning department or municipal government to understand any zoning or home occupation permits required for operating a business from your home.

3. Health and Safety Regulations: Ensure that your home-based laundry operation complies with health and safety regulations. This may include adhering to cleanliness standards, proper sanitation practices, and guidelines for handling laundry chemicals and detergents.

C. *Business Insurance:*

1. Liability Insurance: Consider obtaining general liability insurance to protect your business in case of accidents or incidents that may occur while providing laundry services.

2. Property Insurance: If you invest in specialized equipment for your laundry business, consider property insurance to safeguard your equipment in case of theft, damage, or disasters.

D. *Taxes:*

1. EIN (Employer Identification Number): Depending on your business structure and location, you may need to obtain an EIN from the IRS for tax purposes, even if you don't have employees.

2. Sales Tax: If your locality imposes sales tax on laundry services, you will need to collect and remit this tax to the appropriate

authorities. Check with your state and local tax authorities for their specific requirements.

E. Contracts and Agreements:

1. Customer Agreements: Create clear agreements or terms of service for your customers that outline pricing, service details, payment terms, and any policies regarding lost or damaged items.

2. Supplier Agreements: If you enter into agreements with suppliers for detergents or other laundry supplies, ensure that the terms are clearly defined.

F. Data Protection:

1. Data Handling: If you collect any customer data, such as contact information or payment details, ensure that you are in compliance with data protection regulations, which may include safeguarding sensitive information and obtaining customer consent for data processing.

G. Accessibility and Discrimination Laws:

1. Accessibility: Ensure that your laundry service is accessible to all customers, including those with disabilities. Comply with accessibility laws as applicable to your location.

H. Environmental Regulations:

1. Eco-Friendly Practices: If you promote eco-friendly laundry practices, understand any regulations related to eco-friendly claims and ensure you're using approved environmentally friendly products and methods.

It's essential to consult with legal and regulatory experts or local government authorities to understand the specific legal and regulatory requirements that apply to your home-based laundry business.

Compliance with these requirements not only ensures that your business operates within the law but also enhances your reputation and trustworthiness with customers.

Chapter 3

Home Setup:

The setup of your home-based laundry business is critical for its efficiency and effectiveness. Here are the key aspects to consider:

A. *Designate a Space:*

1. Select an Appropriate Location: Choose a space in your home that is suitable for setting up your laundry business. It could be a dedicated laundry room, garage, or any area that provides adequate space for your equipment and supplies.

2. Space Considerations: Ensure the chosen space is well-ventilated, has proper lighting, and is easily accessible. It should have sufficient electrical outlets for your equipment.

3. Separation from Living Areas: Ideally, separate the laundry area from your living quarters to maintain a clear distinction between your personal space and your business space.

B. Equipment:

1. Washing Machine: Invest in a quality commercial-grade washing machine with a large drum capacity. This will allow you to handle larger loads efficiently.

2. Dryer: A commercial dryer with enough capacity to match your washing machine is essential for drying laundry quickly.

3. Ironing Station: Set up a designated area for ironing with an iron and ironing board to ensure crisp and professional results.

4. Folding and Sorting Area: Allocate space for folding, sorting, and packaging the laundry. Shelves or tables can be used for this purpose.

5. Storage: Arrange storage for detergents, fabric softeners, stain removers, laundry bags, hangers, and other supplies. Organized storage is crucial for maintaining a smooth workflow.

C. Utilities:

1. Water Supply: Ensure a reliable and adequate water supply for your laundry operation. This is particularly important for maintaining the quality and efficiency of your services.

2. Electricity: Verify that the electrical system in your designated laundry area can handle the power requirements of your equipment. Consult an electrician if necessary.

D. Safety Measures:

1. Safety Equipment: Install safety measures like fire extinguishers, smoke detectors, and first-aid kits to ensure the safety of your home and your laundry area.

2. Child Safety: If you have children or pets, take measures to secure your laundry area and ensure they can't access potentially hazardous equipment.

E. Ergonomics:

1. Ergonomic Setup: Arrange your equipment and workspace to minimize physical strain on your body. Consider the height of tables, the arrangement of appliances, and the comfort of your workspace.

F. Aesthetic Considerations:

1. Clean and Tidy: Keep your laundry area clean and organized. A clean and well-maintained workspace reflects professionalism and can boost customer confidence.

G. Maintenance:

1. Regular Maintenance: Schedule regular maintenance for your laundry equipment to ensure they operate efficiently and last longer.

H. Laundry Processes:

1. Establish Workflow: Design an efficient workflow for processing laundry, including sorting, washing, drying, folding, and packaging.

2. Laundry Bags and Identification: Use laundry bags or labels to identify customers' items and keep their laundry separate.

3. Stain Removal Area: Set up a space for stain removal if you offer stain removal as a service.

By paying attention to these home setup considerations, you can create a professional, efficient, and safe space for your home-based laundry business.

The right setup will enhance your business's productivity and customer satisfaction while ensuring that you maintain a balance between your business and personal life within your home.

Chapter 4

Pricing and Services

Determining the right pricing strategy and defining the laundry services you offer are essential steps in running a successful home-based laundry business. Here's how to approach this aspect:

A. Pricing Strategy:

1. Competitive Analysis: Research local competitors and assess their pricing structures. Your prices should be competitive, but they should also allow you to cover your expenses and make a profit.

2. Per-Pound Pricing: Consider charging customers based on the weight of their laundry. This is a straightforward pricing model and is commonly used in laundry services.

3. Service-Specific Pricing: Alternatively, you can offer different pricing for various services such as washing, drying, folding, ironing, and stain removal. This enables customers to customize their orders.

4. Package Deals: Create package deals that bundle multiple services at a discounted rate. For example, offer a package that includes washing, drying, and folding for a set price.

5. Pricing for Pickup and Delivery: If you plan to offer pickup and delivery services, determine the pricing structure for these additional conveniences.

6. Loyalty Programs: Implement loyalty programs or offer discounts to repeat customers to encourage their loyalty and repeat business.

B. Service Options:

1. Laundry Basics: Start by offering fundamental laundry services, including washing, drying, and folding. These services should be the foundation of your offerings.

2. Special Services: Consider additional services such as ironing, stain removal, alterations, and even minor clothing repairs if you have the necessary skills.

3. Eco-Friendly Options: Highlight your eco-friendly practices if you use environmentally friendly detergents and methods. Some customers are willing to pay more for eco-conscious services.

4. Express Service: Offer an express or same-day service for customers who require a quick turnaround. Charge a premium for this service.

5. Customization: Be flexible with customer requests. Allow them to specify their laundry preferences, such as water temperature, detergent types, and folding methods.

6. Discounted Plans: Create subscription or discounted plans for customers who commit to regular or large-scale laundry services.

7. Bulk Orders: Offer special rates for bulk orders, like bedding and large family loads.

C. Communicating Prices:

1. Transparency: Be transparent about your pricing. Provide a clear price list on your website, in your store, or in your marketing materials.

2. Online Quoting: If you have a website, consider including an online quoting tool that allows potential customers to estimate the cost of their laundry.

3. Customer Inquiries: Be prepared to explain your pricing structure to customers and answer any questions they may have.

D. Adjusting Prices:

1. Regular Evaluation: Periodically review your pricing to ensure it remains competitive and covers your costs while allowing you to make a profit.

2. Market Changes: Be prepared to adjust your prices in response to market changes, such as increases in the cost of utilities or supplies.

3. Customer Feedback: Pay attention to customer feedback and reviews to gauge whether your pricing aligns with their expectations and the value they receive.

By establishing a competitive pricing strategy and offering a range of services, you can attract a diverse customer base and maximize your revenue in your home-based laundry business.

Keep in mind that pricing should align with the quality of your service, the convenience you offer, and the unique aspects of your business.

Chapter 5

Marketing and Promotion

Effectively marketing and promoting your home-based laundry business is crucial for attracting customers and building a strong brand presence. Here are key strategies to consider:

A. Branding:

1. Business Name and Logo: Choose a unique, memorable business name and create a professional logo. Your business name and logo should reflect the nature of your services.

2. Brand Identity: Develop a consistent brand identity that includes your business's color scheme, fonts, and visual elements. This identity should be used in all your marketing materials.

B. Online Presence:

1. Website: Create a user-friendly website that showcases your laundry services, pricing, contact information, and any promotions you offer. Include high-quality images of your workspace and satisfied customers.

2. Social Media: Establish a presence on popular social media platforms such as Facebook, Instagram, and Twitter. Share regular updates, customer testimonials, and engaging content related to laundry tips and tricks.

3. Online Booking: If possible, incorporate an online booking system on your website, allowing customers to schedule pickups, deliveries, or services conveniently.

4. Search Engine Optimization (SEO): Optimize your website for search engines to improve its visibility in local search results. Use relevant keywords and phrases, and create content that addresses common laundry-related questions.

C. Local Marketing:

1. Flyers and Brochures: Design and distribute flyers and brochures in your local area. Place them in community centers, local businesses, apartment complexes, and college campuses.

2. Local Ads: Advertise in local newspapers, magazines, or newsletters. Consider sponsoring community events or local sports teams to gain exposure.

3. Referral Programs: Encourage your satisfied customers to refer friends and family by offering referral incentives or discounts.

D. Customer Engagement:

1. Customer Reviews: Encourage customers to leave reviews on your website or on popular review platforms like Google, Yelp, and Facebook. Respond promptly to reviews, both positive and negative, professionally.

2. Email Marketing: Collect customer email addresses and send out regular newsletters with updates, promotions, and helpful laundry tips.

E. Special Promotions and Discounts:

1. Introductory Offers: Attract new customers with introductory discounts or package deals for their first order.

2. Seasonal Promotions: Offer seasonal promotions, such as discounts for spring cleaning, back-to-school specials, or holiday-themed offers.

F. Networking:

1. Local Businesses: Establish partnerships with local businesses like hotels, hostels, and Airbnb hosts to provide laundry services for their guests.

2. Delivery Services: If you offer pickup and delivery, consider partnering with local delivery companies or drivers to expand your reach.

G. Customer Testimonials and Before-After Photos:

1. Showcase Satisfied Customers: Share stories, photos, and testimonials from satisfied customers to build trust and showcase the quality of your services.

H. Regular Updates:

1. Consistent Posting: Maintain a regular posting schedule for your social media accounts and website to keep customers engaged and informed.

2. Content Creation: Share informative and entertaining content related to laundry care, stain removal, and clothing maintenance. This positions you as an expert in the field.

I. Community Involvement:

1. Participate in Local Events: Engage with your community by participating in local events, sponsoring charity drives, or offering free laundry services for community causes.

J. Feedback and Improvement:

1. Customer Feedback: Continuously gather and analyze customer feedback to make improvements to your services and marketing strategies.

Remember that effective marketing is an ongoing effort. Consistency in your branding, messaging, and customer engagement is key to building a strong presence and attracting a loyal customer base for your home-based laundry business.

As you experiment with different marketing strategies, keep a close eye on what works best for your specific market and adapt your approach accordingly.

Chapter 6

Customer Service

Providing exceptional customer service is a fundamental aspect of your home-based laundry business. It can set you apart from competitors and lead to satisfied, loyal customers. Here's how to ensure outstanding customer service:

A. Timeliness and Reliability:

1. Punctuality: Always adhere to agreed-upon schedules for pickups, deliveries, and services. Timeliness is essential to earn and maintain trust.

2. Consistency: Be consistent in your service offerings and quality. Customers should know what to expect each time they use your laundry service.

B. Quality Service:

1. Garment Care: Pay attention to garment care labels and instructions to ensure that clothing is handled appropriately. Use the right washing cycles and detergents to prevent damage.

2. Stain Removal: Invest time and effort in effective stain removal techniques. Succeeding in this area can impress customers and lead to word-of-mouth recommendations.

C. Communication:

1. Clear Communication: Maintain clear and prompt communication with customers. Answer queries, provide order updates, and address any concerns professionally.

2. Feedback Channels: Encourage customers to provide feedback through surveys or reviews. Act on their feedback to improve your services.

D. Problem Resolution:

1. Customer Complaints: Handle customer complaints and issues with care and professionalism. Resolve problems promptly and strive for a fair resolution.

2. Customer Satisfaction: Ensure that customers are satisfied with the resolution to their concerns. This could turn a negative experience into a positive one.

E. Personalized Service:

1. Know Your Customers: Build relationships with regular customers. Remember their preferences, special requests, and any notes they've provided in the past.

2. Customization: Offer customization options, such as varying water temperatures, detergents, or folding methods, to accommodate individual preferences.

F. Service Transparency:

1. Pricing Transparency: Clearly communicate your pricing structure and any additional charges. Customers appreciate transparency in financial transactions.

2. Laundry Handling: Inform customers about how you handle their laundry. Assure them of confidentiality and security.

G. Accessibility:

1. Communication Channels: Offer multiple means of communication, such as phone, email, and social media. Make sure you are accessible to address customer inquiries and issues.

2. Accessibility for All: Ensure that your laundry services are accessible to people with disabilities. Make reasonable accommodations as needed.

H. Customer Appreciation:

1. Loyalty Programs: Implement loyalty programs that reward repeat customers with discounts, exclusive promotions, or free services after a certain number of orders.

2. Thank-You Notes: Express appreciation for your customers by including personalized thank-you notes with their orders.

I. Professional Presentation:

1. Clean and Tidy: Maintain a clean, tidy workspace. Your laundry area should reflect professionalism, order, and hygiene.

2. Uniforms: Consider wearing professional uniforms or attire when meeting customers for pickups and deliveries.

J. Repeat Business:

1. Retention Strategies: Develop strategies to retain customers. Keep them engaged through newsletters, special offers, and follow-ups after services.

2. Customer Feedback: Actively seek customer feedback to identify areas for improvement and show your commitment to their satisfaction.

K. Safety and Security:

1. Data Protection: Safeguard customer data, such as contact information and payment details, to protect their privacy and comply with data protection regulations.

2. Safety Measures: Prioritize safety with measures like fire extinguishers, smoke detectors, and first-aid kits in your home-based laundry area.

L. Eco-Friendly Practices:

1. Environmental Responsibility: Communicate your eco-friendly practices and initiatives to attract environmentally conscious customers.

Exceptional customer service is the cornerstone of a successful laundry business. When customers receive high-quality, reliable, and personalized service, they are more likely to become repeat clients and recommend your business to others.

Continuously seek ways to improve your customer service, as it's an ongoing process that can set you apart in a competitive market.

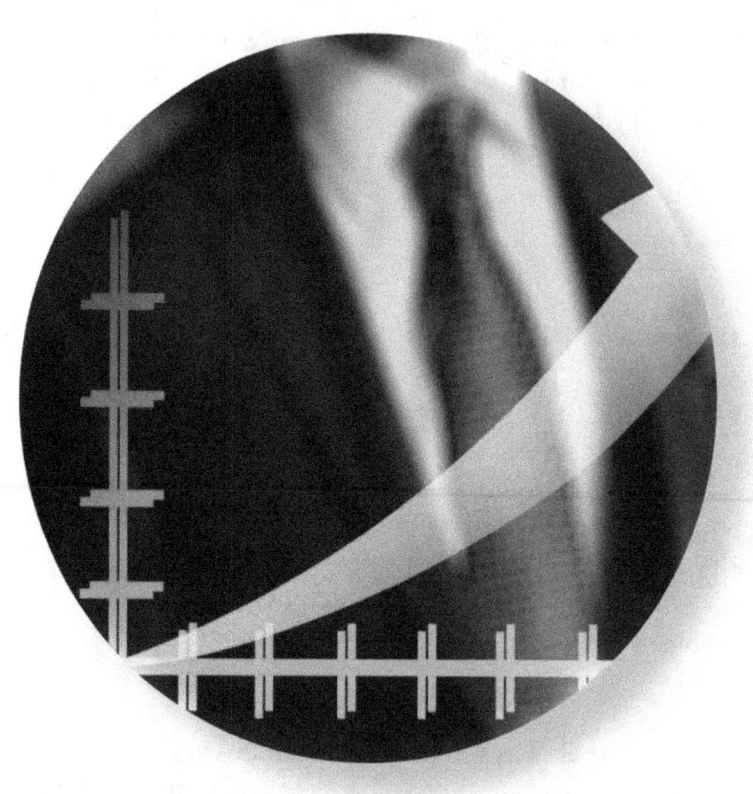

Chapter 7

Record Keeping and Finances

Proper financial management and accurate record-keeping are crucial for the success and sustainability of your home-based laundry business. Here's how to manage this aspect effectively:

A. Expense Tracking:

1. Create Categories: Organize your expenses into categories, such as equipment costs, utilities, supplies, marketing, and permits. This structured approach will make it easier to track your spending.

2. Receipts and Invoices: Keep all receipts, invoices, and financial documents in an organized manner. Consider using digital tools or software to store and manage these records.

3. Expense Log: Maintain a detailed expense log that records each transaction, the date, amount, and purpose. This log helps you understand where your money is going.

B. Income Recording:

1. Sales Tracking: Keep a comprehensive record of all your sales. This should include the date of each transaction, the customer's name, the services provided, and the amount earned.

2. Invoice Generation: Issue invoices to your customers for services rendered. Please make sure to provide all essential information, including the dates by which payments are due and the methods of payment that are accepted.

C. Accounting Software:

1. Use Accounting Software: Consider using accounting software or tools like QuickBooks or FreshBooks to help manage your finances more efficiently. These tools can automate many tasks and provide valuable financial insights.

2. Accountant Services: If your business grows or you find managing finances challenging, consider hiring an accountant or bookkeeper to help with record-keeping, tax preparation, and financial analysis.

D. Tax Obligations:

1. Tax Records: Maintain thorough tax records, including information related to income, expenses, and deductions. Ensure that you're prepared to fulfill your tax obligations at the local, state, and federal levels.

2. Tax Filing: Comply with tax filing deadlines and seek professional guidance to maximize deductions and minimize tax liability.

E. Budgeting:

1. Financial Projections: Develop a budget and financial projections that outline your expected income and expenses. Use these projections to set financial goals and plan for growth.

2. Monitoring and Adjusting: Regularly monitor your budget and make adjustments as needed. This enables you to stay on track and make well informed financial decisions.

F. Business Bank Account:

1. Separate Accounts: Maintain a separate business bank account to ensure that personal and business finances are distinct. This streamlines the process of maintaining records and aids in adhering to tax regulations.

G. Payment Processing:

1. Accept Multiple Payment Methods: Offer various payment methods to accommodate your customers. This might include cash, credit cards, online payments, or mobile payment apps.

2. Payment Reconciliation: Reconcile your payments with your sales records to ensure that all income is accurately recorded.

H. Financial Reports:

1. Regular Reporting: Generate and review financial reports regularly, such as profit and loss statements, balance sheets, and cash flow statements. These reports offer valuable information about the financial well-being of your company.

2. Forecasting: Use financial reports and forecasts to make informed decisions about pricing, marketing strategies, and business expansion.

I. Savings and Emergency Fund:

1. Set Aside Funds: Allocate a portion of your income to savings and create an emergency fund to cover unexpected expenses or business downturns.

J. Debt Management:

1. Debt Record: Keep track of any business loans, credit card balances, or other debts. Ensure that you're making timely payments and managing debt responsibly.

Accurate record-keeping and sound financial management are essential for making informed decisions, tracking the health of your business, and meeting your financial obligations.

Regularly review and update your financial records to ensure the continued success and sustainability of your home-based laundry business.

Chapter 8

Eco-Friendly Practices

Incorporating eco-friendly practices into your home-based laundry business not only helps the environment but can also attract environmentally conscious customers who value sustainability. Here's how to integrate eco-friendly practices:

A. Green Detergents and Chemicals:

1. Eco-Friendly Products: Opt for environmentally friendly and biodegradable detergents, fabric softeners, and stain removers. These products are less harmful to the environment and often safer for customers with sensitivities.

2. Low-Impact Chemicals: Use chemicals that have a low impact on water quality and the ecosystem, such as detergents with the EPA's Safer Choice label

B. Energy Efficiency:

1. Energy-Efficient Appliances: Invest in energy-efficient washing machines and dryers. These machines use less water and electricity, reducing your carbon footprint.

2. Cold Water Wash: Encourage customers to use cold water for washing whenever possible. It saves energy and helps preserve the integrity of clothing.

C. Water Conservation:

1. Water-Saving Practices: Implement water-saving measures, such as fixing leaks, using front-loading machines (which use less water), and reusing water for multiple loads when feasible.

2. Rainwater Harvesting: If you're in a location with regular rainfall, consider collecting and using rainwater for certain laundry processes.

D. Packaging and Supplies:

1. Reusable Packaging: Use reusable laundry bags or containers for pickups and deliveries, reducing the need for single-use plastic bags.

2. Recycled Materials: Choose packaging materials made from recycled or biodegradable materials. For example, use paper bags or cardboard boxes instead of plastic.

3. Eco-Friendly Hangers: If you offer hanger services, consider using recycled or sustainable materials for hangers.

E. Promote Sustainable Practices:

1. Educate Customers: Educate your customers about the benefits of eco-friendly laundry practices and the importance of reducing water and energy consumption.

2. Rewards for Sustainability: Offer incentives to customers who adopt eco-friendly practices, such as using cold water for washing or requesting minimal packaging.

F. Sustainable Facility:

1. Eco-Friendly Workspace: Implement sustainable practices in your laundry area. This may include using energy-efficient lighting, insulating your workspace for better temperature control, and ensuring proper ventilation.

2. Recycling and Waste Management: Set up a recycling program for materials like cardboard, paper, and plastics. Properly dispose of hazardous waste, such as detergent containers, following local regulations.

G. Carbon Offset:

1. Offset Emissions: Consider participating in carbon offset programs to compensate for any carbon emissions your business generates. These programs invest in projects that reduce greenhouse gases.

H. Certifications and Partnerships:

1. Eco-Certifications: Seek certifications that reflect your commitment to eco-friendly practices, such as being a Green Business or achieving the Green Seal certification.

2. Partnerships: Collaborate with suppliers and partners who share your eco-friendly values and provide sustainable products and services.

I. Marketing Eco-Friendly Practices:

1. Highlight Your Commitment: Showcase your commitment to eco-friendly practices on your website, social media, and marketing materials. Let customers know that their choice supports a green business.

2. Eco-Friendly Branding: Incorporate eco-friendly messaging and imagery into your branding to reinforce your commitment to sustainability.

By incorporating eco-friendly practices into your home-based laundry business, you can attract environmentally conscious customers, reduce your environmental impact, and contribute to a more sustainable future.

Moreover, these practices can set your business apart in a competitive market by aligning with growing consumer demands for sustainability.

Chapter 9

Networking

Networking in the context of your home-based laundry business involves building relationships and connections with individuals and organizations that can help your business grow and thrive.

Effective networking can open up opportunities, provide support, and increase your business's visibility. Here's how to engage in networking:

A. Local Businesses:

1. Laundry Equipment Suppliers: Establish connections with local suppliers of laundry equipment, detergents, and supplies. These suppliers can offer you competitive prices and keep you updated on the latest products.

2. Dry Cleaners and Laundromats: Forge relationships with nearby dry cleaners and laundromats. They can be a source of referrals when customers have laundry needs that they can't handle.

3. Local Chambers of Commerce: Join your local chamber of commerce or small business association. These organizations often provide networking events and resources for small business owners.

4. Local Retailers: Collaborate with local clothing retailers to provide laundry and garment care services for their merchandise.

B. Delivery Services:

1. Local Couriers: If you offer pickup and delivery services, establish relationships with local courier services or delivery drivers. They can assist with logistics and expand your reach.

C. Online Networking:

1. Social Media: Connect with potential customers and other businesses through social media platforms. Engage with relevant groups and forums in your niche.

2. Online Forums and Communities: Participate in online forums and communities related to laundry, entrepreneurship, or small business ownership. Share your knowledge with others and learn from them.

3. LinkedIn: Create a professional LinkedIn profile for your business. Connect with professionals in your industry, potential customers, and suppliers.

D. Collaborative Partnerships:

1. Hotels and Hostels: Form partnerships with local hotels, hostels, and Airbnb hosts to provide laundry services to their guests.

2. Event Planners: Collaborate with event planners for weddings, conferences, and other events. They may require laundry services for linens, uniforms, and decorations.

E. Local Events:

1. Community Events: Participate in community events and fairs. Set up a booth to promote your laundry services and engage with potential customers.

2. Laundry Workshops: Offer free or paid laundry workshops to the community. This can showcase your expertise and build trust.

F. Referral Programs:

1. Customer Referrals: Encourage satisfied customers to refer friends and family to your laundry services. Consider offering discounts or rewards for successful referrals.

G. Business Networking Groups:

1. Business Networking Events: Attend local business networking events and meetups to connect with fellow entrepreneurs, exchange ideas, and discover opportunities for collaboration.

H. Online Marketplaces:

1. Online Platforms: List your services on online marketplaces or directories related to laundry and cleaning services. These platforms can help you reach a broader customer base.

I. Local Advertising:

1. Local Magazines and Newsletters: Advertise your business in local magazines, newspapers, and newsletters. This can increase your visibility in the community.

2. Sponsorships: Sponsor local events, teams, or charitable causes. This can boost your brand's presence and reputation in the area.

Effective networking can lead to partnerships, collaborations, and a broader customer base for your home-based laundry business. It's essential to approach networking with a genuine interest in building relationships and offering value to others.

 As you develop your network, you'll discover opportunities to grow and improve your business while contributing to the local community.

Chapter 10.

Expansion

Expanding your home-based laundry business involves increasing your reach, services, or capacity to serve a larger customer base or explore new opportunities.

Expansion is a significant step that can lead to business growth and increased revenue. Here are some ways to consider expansion:

A. Service Expansion:

1. Add New Services: Diversify your laundry services by offering additional options like dry cleaning, ironing, alterations, or specialized fabric care.

2. Eco-Friendly Services: If you haven't already, introduce eco-friendly laundry practices to cater to environmentally conscious customers.

3. Specialized Services: Explore niche markets like pet laundry, baby clothing care, or delicate fabric cleaning.

4. Bulk Orders: Target larger customers, such as local businesses or institutions, and offer bulk laundry services.

B. Geographic Expansion:

1. Wider Service Area: Expand your service area to cover more neighborhoods or nearby towns. This may require additional pickup and delivery resources.

2. Online Presence: Promote your services to a wider audience through online platforms and social media, reaching customers beyond your immediate vicinity.

C. Pickup and Delivery:

1. Extended Hours: Offer extended pickup and delivery hours to accommodate a broader customer base.

2. Additional Vehicles: If demand is high, consider investing in more vehicles to increase your delivery capacity.

D. Physical Expansion:

1. Larger Space: If your current laundry setup is limited, consider moving to a larger location or expanding your existing space to handle more laundry loads.

2. Commercial Space: Transition from a home-based operation to a commercial space to increase your capacity and professional image.

E. Franchising:

1. Franchise Model: Consider franchising your laundry business. This allows others to replicate your successful business model in different locations, expanding your brand's reach.

F. Marketing and Promotion:

1. Marketing Strategies: Implement targeted marketing strategies to attract new customers and keep existing ones engaged. This can include digital marketing, advertising, and promotions.

2. Customer Referrals: Encourage customer referrals to reach a wider audience and reward customers who bring in new business.

G. Technology Integration:

1. Online Booking System: Invest in an online booking system to streamline customer interactions and improve convenience.

2. Delivery Apps: Consider developing a dedicated app for pickup and delivery services to make ordering more convenient for customers.

H. Partnerships and Collaborations:

1. Collaborate with Local Businesses: Partner with local businesses, such as hotels, event planners, or schools, to provide laundry services for their specific needs.

2. Supply Chain Partners: Strengthen relationships with suppliers and negotiate better deals as your order volumes increase.

I. Financial Planning:

1. Secure Funding: If necessary, explore funding options like business loans or grants to support your expansion plans.

2. Financial Projections: Create detailed financial projections to estimate the costs and potential returns associated with your expansion.

J. Staffing:

1. Hiring Employees: As your business grows, consider hiring employees to help with laundry operations, deliveries, customer service, and administrative tasks.

K. Regulatory Compliance:

1. Check Regulations: Be aware of any additional permits, licenses, or regulatory requirements that may come with business expansion, especially if you're changing your location or adding new services.

Expanding your home-based laundry business requires careful planning, including market research, financial analysis, and operational adjustments. Ensure that your business is prepared for expansion by having the necessary infrastructure, resources, and a clear strategy in place.

Expansion can be an exciting opportunity to take your business to new heights and serve a broader customer base.

CONCLUSION

As you reach the final chapter of "The Laundry Entrepreneur: A Guide to Launching Your Home-Based Laundry Business with Minimal Capital," I hope you've found inspiration, guidance, and the motivation to turn your laundry business dreams into reality. Your entrepreneurial journey is about to unfold, and the possibilities are as vast as the piles of laundry waiting to be transformed.

In concluding our exploration, remember that success in the laundry business, like any venture, is a journey, not just a destination. The lessons you've gleaned from these pages—whether about efficient operations, customer satisfaction, or the power of innovation—serve as stepping stones toward your entrepreneurial aspirations.

As you embark on this exciting path, keep in mind the resilience and adaptability that define successful entrepreneurs. Your laundry business is more than just washing and folding; it's a testament to your creativity, tenacity, and ability to see opportunities where others might see challenges.

In the world of entrepreneurship, every setback is a setup for a comeback. Learn from your experiences, adapt to the ever-changing market, and embrace the challenges as opportunities to refine your skills and strategies. Your journey may not always be smooth, but it's the twists and turns that make the story truly compelling.

As you launch your home-based laundry business with minimal capital, remember that success is not solely measured in monetary gains. It's also about the satisfaction of building something from the ground up, the joy of satisfied customers, and the pride of being your own boss. Celebrate each milestone, no matter how small, and use setbacks as stepping stones to greater achievements.

In closing, may your laundry business flourish, your entrepreneurial spirit soar, and your journey be filled with the sweet aroma of success. As you navigate the twists and turns of entrepreneurship, always remember that the passion you bring to your business is the most potent detergent for achieving lasting success.

Best of luck on your entrepreneurial odyssey, and may your home-based laundry business be a shining beacon of what can be achieved with determination, innovation, and a dash of entrepreneurial spirit!

JEFFREY FERON

Author

Meknatureconcept@gmail.com.

www.ingramcontent.com/pod-product-compliance
Lightning Source LLC
Chambersburg PA
CBHW062253290526
45794CB00006B/2531